Living Lights

Bernadette Kelly

Contents

It Glows!

Some living things can make their own light. These "living lights" glow brightly in the dark.

The ocean is full of living things that glow. On land, only a few living things glow.

Animals glow for different reasons. Some animals glow to help them catch other animals to eat. Some animals glow to help them hide from other animals that want to eat them!

Other things can glow too. This **fungus** is glowing.

The light from an animal can also be a type of signal. It is a way to **attract** other animals.

The anglerfish has a light on the end of its spine to attract prey.

Would you like to see some living lights? Come with me. I'll light the way.

Glow Worms

Glow worms are living lights. Glow worms live in dark caves and **rainforests** in many parts of the world.

Did You Know?

Glow worms are not really worms! They are baby insects (larvae) or adult female insects that glow.

This cave glitters with glow worms.

Female glow worms have a light at the end of their tail. The light attracts male glow worms.

Fireflies

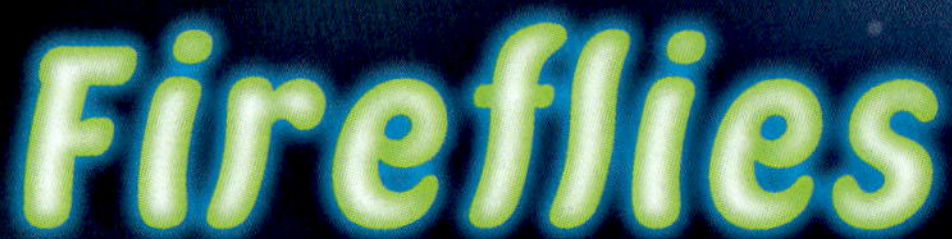

Fireflies can glow, too. There are more than 2000 types of fireflies. They can be found all over the world.

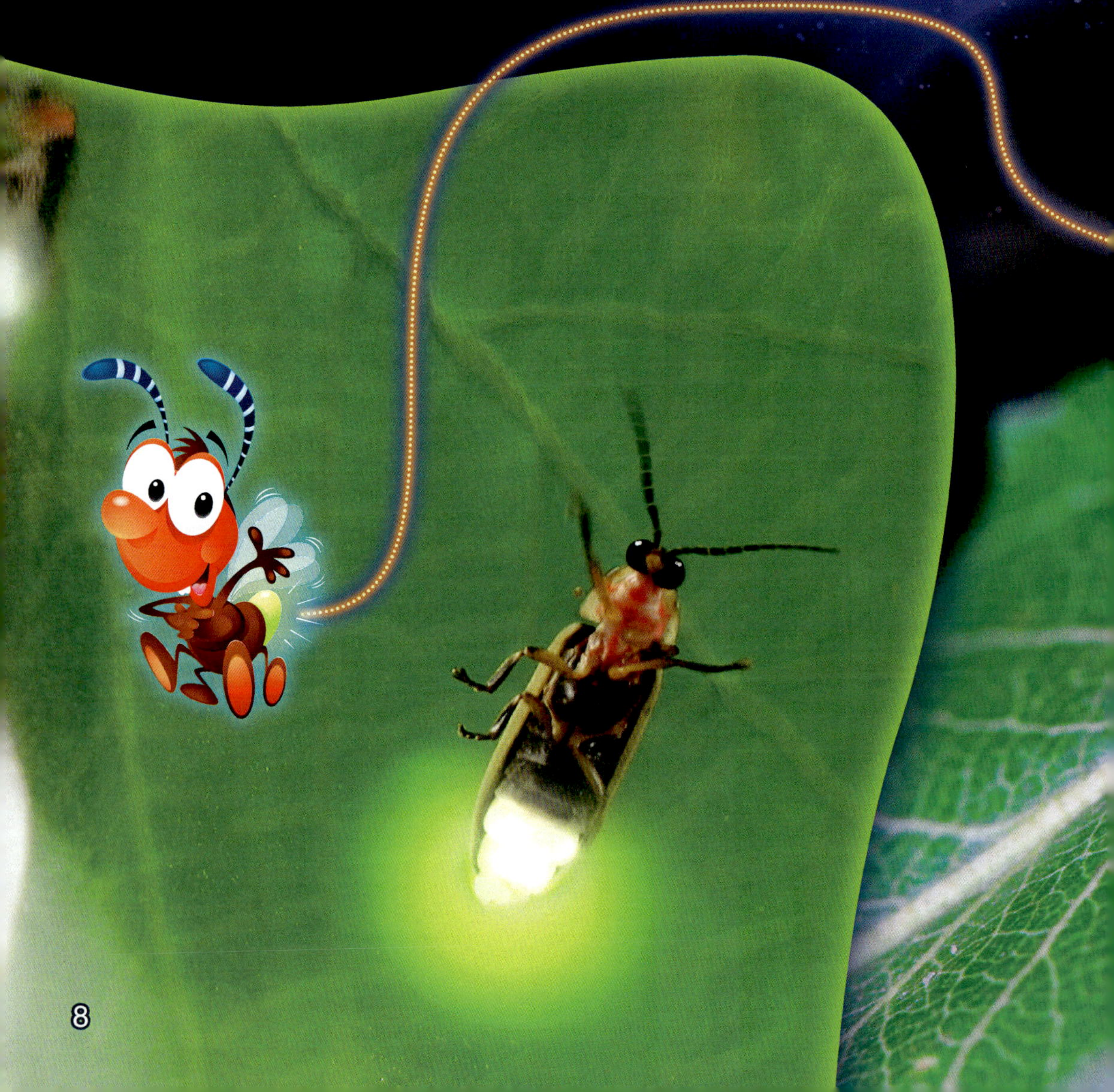

A firefly's light can be yellow, green or orange. They talk to each other by flashing their light on and off.

Did You Know?

Fireflies are not really flies at all. They are beetles. Sometimes, they are called lightning bugs.

Fungi

It is not just animals that can glow. Some fungi, like mushrooms, can glow as well.

There is a special fungi that grows on **rotting** wood in forests. It makes a blue-green glow. This glow is called "foxfire".

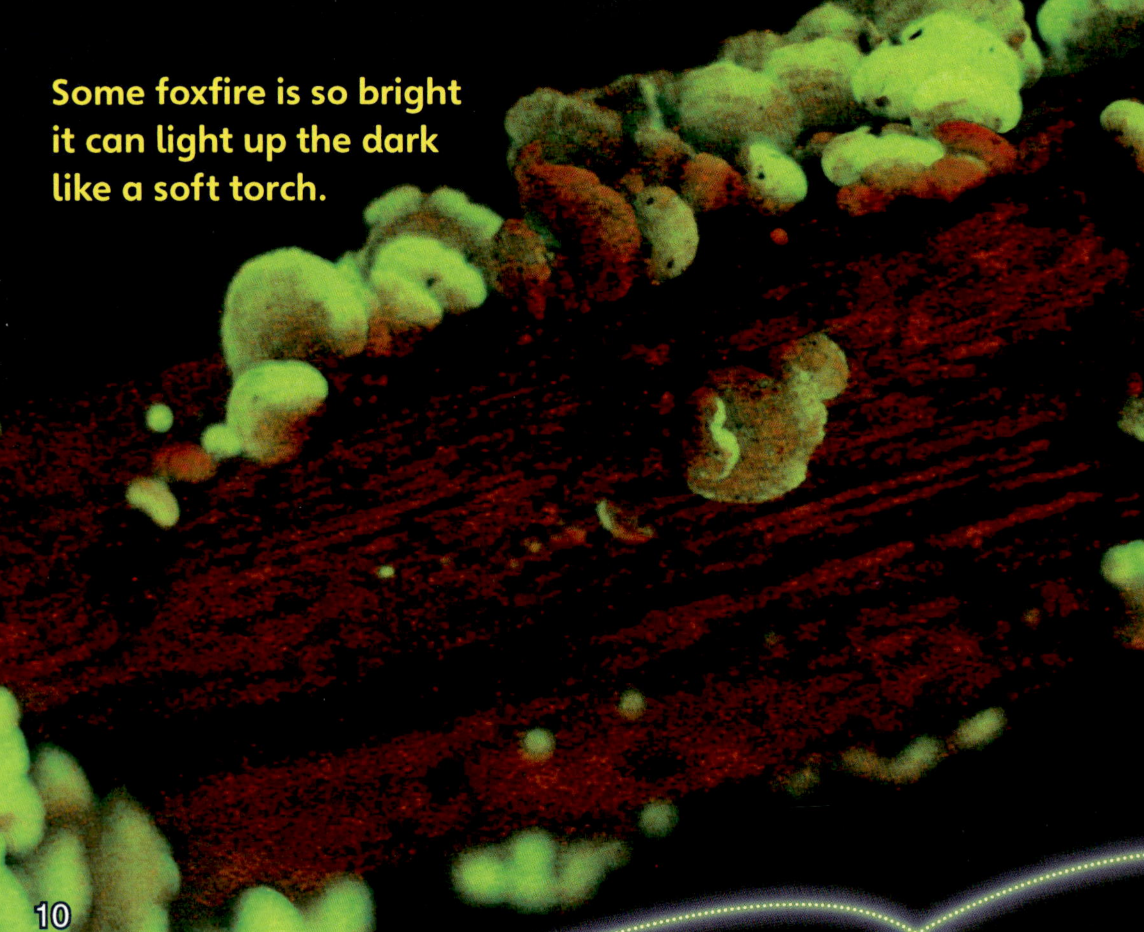

Some foxfire is so bright it can light up the dark like a soft torch.

There are mushrooms called jack-o-lanterns that glow brightly in the forest, too.

Did You Know?

Jack-o-lantern mushrooms are very poisonous, so never eat one!

Algae

Algae are a large group of living things that look like plants. They usually live in the sea.

Don't swim here! The sea is full of red algae.

Sometimes, glowing algae grows close together. This is called an algal bloom. Algal blooms can be green, red or brown.

Did You Know?

Often, red algal blooms glow blue at night.

Jellyfish

Some animals that glow live deep in the ocean. Jellyfish are the most common type of glowing animal.

Jellyfish usually glow with blue light, but sometimes they glow green or red.

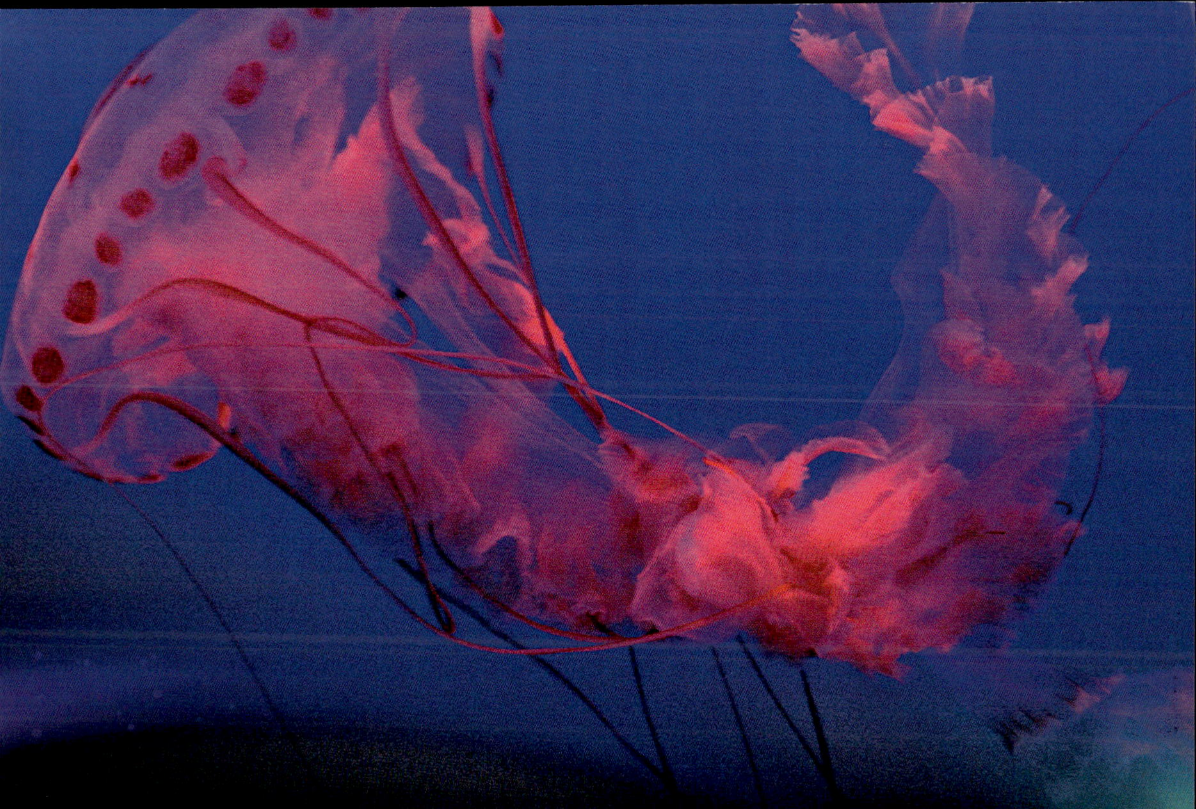

Some jellyfish glow to warn off other animals who might want to eat them. They also glow to help catch food, such as fish. Fish are attracted to the light and are caught in the long stinging tentacles (arms) of the jellyfish.

Squid

Some squid can glow, too. Squid are animals that live in the sea and have a head and a set of arms or tentacles.

The giant squid has lights on its tentacles.

Did You Know?

A squid's eyes are always open because they have no eyelids.

Squid use their glowing lights to hide from other animals. They match their own light to the light in the water. This means that animals swimming below cannot see them.

Fish

Some fish that glow live deep in the ocean.

The anglerfish lives in oceans all over the world. It has a large head with one or two thin spikes called spines that hang over its eyes.

Anglerfish can wiggle their spines to help them attract fish to eat.

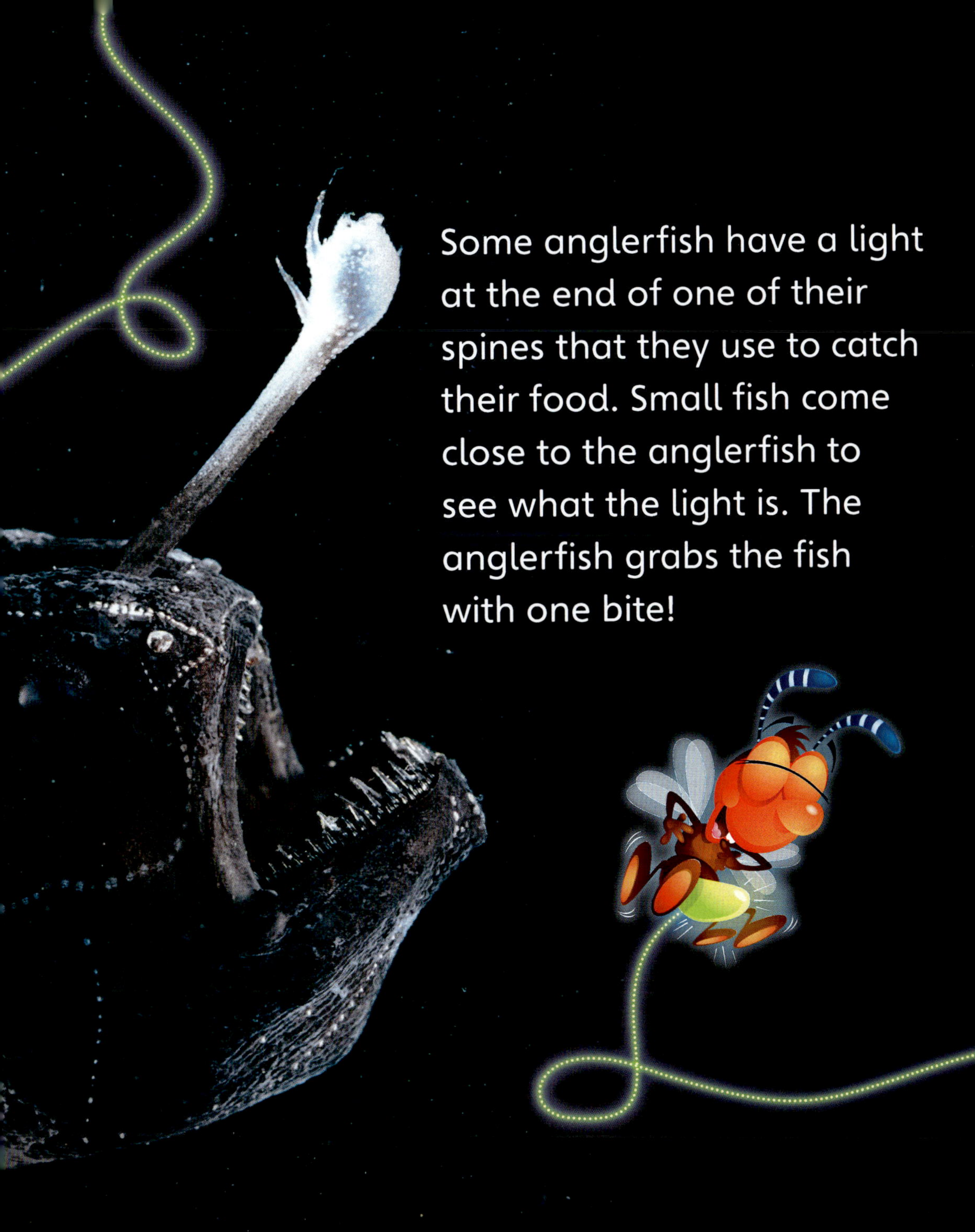

Some anglerfish have a light at the end of one of their spines that they use to catch their food. Small fish come close to the anglerfish to see what the light is. The anglerfish grabs the fish with one bite!

Sharks

The cookiecutter shark is a living light, too. It lives in warm ocean waters all over the world.

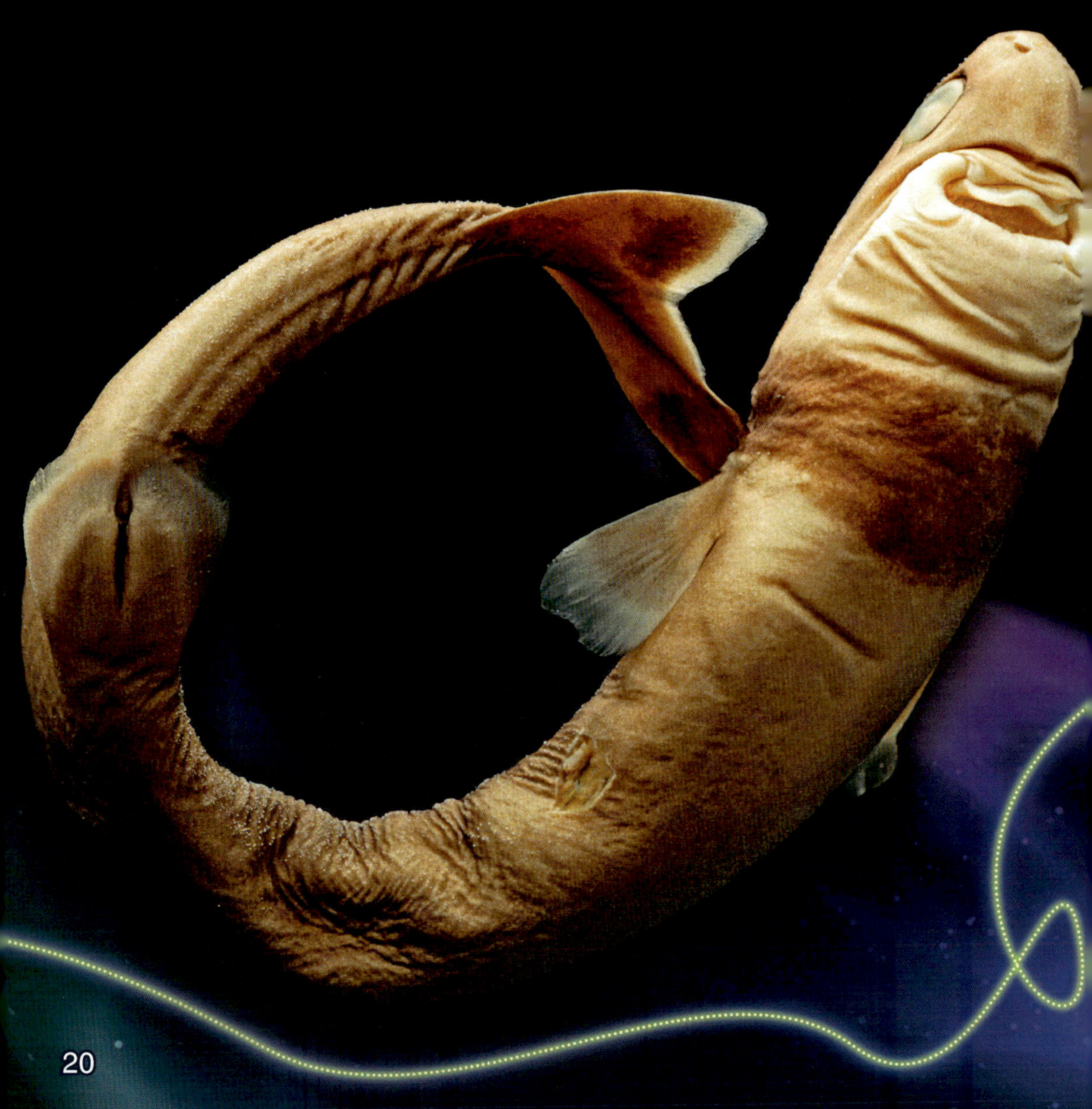

This shark uses its light to hide and to catch food. All of the shark's underside glows except for a dark patch near its head. Bigger fish think the dark patch is a little fish and try to eat it but the cookiecutter bites them instead.

Did You Know?

The cookiecutter shark gets its name from the way it eats. It chews round chunks out of the animals it eats!

Living Lights

Did you enjoy exploring living lights? Things that glow in the dark can be fascinating and lots of fun, too!

Well, I'm off now. See you later!

Glossary

attract	to make someone or something interested
fungus	a living thing that is neither plant nor animal, such as mushrooms
prey	living thing that is food for other living things
rainforests	forests in warm, wet areas
rotting	slowly breaking down, decaying

Index